THE
LIFE OF
JESUS

Bible Stories, Poems and Prayers

SELECTED AND RETOLD BY
ANN PILLING

ILLUSTRATED BY
KADY MACDONALD DENTON

Kingfisher

For David and Lorna, Lydia and
Naomi, with much love   A.P.

For Gina Pollinger   K.M.D.

KINGFISHER
An imprint of Larousse plc
Elsley House, 24-30 Great Titchfield Street
London W1P 7AD

This paperback edition first published by Kingfisher 1996
2 4 6 8 10 9 7 5 3 1

Material in this edition was previously
published by Kingfisher in 1990 in *Before I Go to Sleep*

A CIP catalogue record for this book
is available from the British Library.

ISBN 0 7534 0004 9

Printed in Hong Kong

For permission to reproduce copyright material, acknowledgement and thanks
are due to Church Mission Society for "Lord of the loving heart";
HarperCollins Publishers Ltd for "Once upon a time there was a man who
was a miracle" from *The Golden Cockerel Book of Morning Readings* by M.E. Rose
and for "Bread" by Freda Elton Young from *The Book of a Thousand Poems*
selected by H.E. Wilkinson; SCM Press for "A Prayer from Prison" by
Dietrich Bonhoeffer from *Letters and Papers from Prison* 1971.
Extracts from the Authorized Version of the Bible (The King James Bible), the
rights in which are vested in the Crown, are reproduced by permission of the
Crown's Patentee, Cambride University Press. New English Bible copyright ©
Oxford Unversity Press and Cambridge University Press 1961, 1970.

CONTENTS

I Sing of a Maiden

I sing of a maiden
That is makeless;*
King of all kings
To her son she chose.

He came all so still
Where his mother was,
As dew in April
That falleth on the grass.

He came all so still
To his mother's bower,
As dew in April
That falleth on the flower.

He came all so still
Where his mother lay,
As dew in April
That falleth on the spray.

Mother and maiden
Was never none but she;
Well may such a lady
God's mother be.

*matchless   *Unknown*

MARY

There was once a young girl called Mary. She lived in Galilee in a town called Nazareth and she was soon to marry a carpenter called Joseph.

But one day God sent Gabriel, the greatest angel of all, to give her some very important news. She was troubled when she saw him, and wondered what on earth he could want with her.

"Greetings, most favoured one," he said, "and do not be afraid. You have found favour with God. Very soon you are going to have a baby. You must call him Jesus. He will be great, the Son of the Most High. God will give him the throne of David, his mighty ancestor, and he will reign for ever and ever."

But Mary was puzzled. "I am not even married," she told the angel.

"The Holy Spirit will come down to you," Gabriel said, "and God's own power will rest upon you; therefore, that holy thing which you shall bear will be called the Son of God. Nothing is impossible with him."

"I am his servant," Mary whispered. "May it happen just as you have said." And Gabriel went away.

But when she was alone she lifted up her voice and rejoiced.

"Tell out, my soul, the greatness of the Lord,
Rejoice, O my soul, in God my Saviour,
Who has looked so tenderly upon his humble servant.
For from this day all people shall call me 'blessed',
The Lord has dealt with me so wonderfully."

Luke 1.

NO ROOM

Just a few days before her baby was born, Mary had to go on a long journey with the carpenter Joseph. Everyone had been ordered to pay a special tax in their home town, and his home was in Bethlehem.

Just as they arrived, Mary knew that her baby was going to be born; but there was no room for them in the inn. All they were offered was a stable, and that is where the Son of God was born. There was no lovely silk-lined cot for him, only a manger full of hay, with the animals standing around.

That night some shepherds, who were out guarding their sheep on the hills near Bethlehem, were startled by a great light in the sky. An angel came down and told them not to be afraid. "I bring you good news of great joy," he said, "news

for everyone on earth. Christ the Lord has been born tonight. If you go now, you will find him wrapped in swaddling clothes, lying in a manger."

And suddenly the whole sky was filled with angels, hundreds upon thousands of them, all praising God. "Glory to God in the highest," they sang, "and on earth peace, good will towards all people."

"Come on," the shepherds said to each other, when at last the angels had gone away. "Let's go to Bethlehem and see for ourselves." So they rushed off and found Mary and Joseph, and baby Jesus lying in a manger, exactly as the angel had said.

Luke 2.

THE THREE KINGS

Meanwhile, in his great palace in Jerusalem, jealous King Herod had been talking to some wise men. He was alarmed, and frightened, because he had heard about the baby that had been born in Bethlehem and he feared that the child would one day seize his throne. The prophets had said that a great king, the 'Messiah', would be born in that little town.

"Where is this baby who is going to be King of the Jews?" the wise men asked Herod. "We have seen his special star in the east and we want to go and worship him."

"You'll find him in Bethlehem," Herod said. Then he added cunningly, "But be sure to let me know when you get there. I want to come and worship him too."

So off they went, following the star; and it led them all the way to Bethlehem where it stopped, hovering over the place where Jesus lay. They were overjoyed to see the star there and they went straight in. Out of their great store of treasures they gave the baby gifts, gold and frankincense and myrrh. But they were not so foolish as to return to Herod. In a dream God had warned them to find a different way home.

In another dream, God gave a warning to Joseph. "Go to Egypt," his angel said, "and stay there till I tell you all is safe. King Herod is plotting to kill your baby son."

So Joseph got up immediately and stole away by night with Mary and their child, for the far-off land of Egypt.

Herod flew into a great rage when he realized that the wise men had tricked him. He gave a cruel command that all the young children in and around Bethlehem should be killed. That way he could be sure that Jesus would die too.

But Joseph and Mary were already safe in Egypt, and they did not go back again until Herod was dead and they knew it was safe. Then they settled in the town of Nazareth, with Jesus.

God was looking after his precious son most carefully; he was going to do such wonderful things when he grew up.

Matthew 2.

DEAR GOD, we thank you that your tiny son,
born in a stable, had a heart big enough
to embrace the whole world. AMEN

Ann Pilling

10

Jesus in Trouble

When Jesus was twelve years old, Mary and Joseph went up to Jerusalem as usual, for the great feast of the Passover, and took their son with them. When it was all over, they set off for home again, travelling with a big group of friends; but Jesus stayed behind. They had gone a whole day's journey before they realized he was missing. Then they began to hunt anxiously amongst all their friends and relations. But Jesus was nowhere to be found.

Off they trudged, all the way back to Jerusalem. But it was a big, bustling city and they spent three days looking for him. Finally they spotted him in the Temple, sitting in the middle of all the Jewish teachers, asking all kind of questions and listening carefully to their answers. Everyone who heard him was amazed at his deep understanding, and at how much such a young boy knew.

His parents were astonished to find him there, and Mary could not hide her distress. "My son," she said, "why have you treated us like this? Your father and I have been terribly worried; we've looked everywhere for you."

"But why did you look for me?" Jesus asked them calmly. "Didn't you know that I had to be in my Father's house, doing my Father's work?" But neither of his parents understood what he was saying.

Together, they all returned home to Nazareth, and after this their young son was much more obedient. But Mary never forgot what had happened in the temple, treasuring the memory in her heart.

As for Jesus, he grew taller and stronger, and he grew in wisdom too. People loved him, but nobody loved him as much as his Father in heaven, in whose house he had lingered when he was just twelve years old.

Luke 2.

MY BEST FRIEND

Jesus, friend of little children,
    Be a friend to me
Take my hand and ever keep me
    Close to thee.

Teach me how to grow in goodness,
    Daily as I grow:
Thou hast been a child, and surely
    Thou dost know.

Never leave me, nor forsake me;
    Ever be my friend;
For I need thee, from life's dawning
    To its end.

Walter J. Mathams

A Marvellous Picnic

Everybody wanted to meet Jesus, and to hear his wonderful stories, and wherever he went huge crowds followed him. Once, when he had been preaching all day, he said to his special friends, the disciples, "Let us go away by ourselves now, to some lonely place, so that you can all get some rest." So they set off in a boat to find somewhere really quiet and peaceful.

But the people had all rushed ahead of them and the minute Jesus stepped on shore everybody crowded round eagerly. His heart filled with love for them then; they were like sheep who had lost their shepherd, and although he was very tired he started preaching again.

The day wore on and on and his friends began to worry. "It's getting late," they said, "and this is such a lonely place. Send the people away now to the villages round about, to buy themselves something to eat."

"You feed them," Jesus replied.

"How on earth can we buy food for so many?" one of them wanted to know. "There must be about five thousand people here." Then another came up and said, "There's a lad here, Master, with five barley loaves and two fish. But that won't go very far."

"Make everybody sit down," Jesus commanded, so they all settled themselves on the grassy slopes in little groups.

Then he took the loaves and the fish, looked up to heaven and gave thanks, then passed the food to his disciples to give to the hungry people. Everyone ate till they were quite satisfied and at the end of the meal there were enough crumbs and bits of fish left over to fill twelve baskets. It was the most marvellous picnic ever.

I think that boy with the loaves and the fish must have remembered it all his life, don't you?

Matthew 14; Mark 6; Luke 9; John 6.

Bread

Be gentle when you touch Bread.
Let it not lie
Uncared for,
Unwanted.
So often Bread
Is taken for granted.

Beauty of patient toil,
Wind and rain
Have caressed it.
Christ often blessed it.
Be gentle when you touch Bread.

Freda Elton Young

THE BIG STORM

On the day of the marvellous picnic it was late in the afternoon when Jesus finally sent the people away. He told the disciples to get into their boat and sail home ahead of him, while he went into the hills to pray.

When evening came he was still alone. The boat was a long way from land by this time, and a really bad storm had blown up. The waves were crashing against the side of the boat, and the wind was howling. All night, the disciples had to struggle to hold their course.

Very early next morning, long before sunrise, Jesus came to find them, walking across the water. When they saw what he was doing they cried out in terror, "It's a ghost." But he calmed them at once, saying, "Take heart, it is I. Do not be afraid."

Peter, his chief disciple, said, "Lord, if it really *is* you, command me to walk on the sea as well."

"All right," Jesus replied. "Come," and he held out his hand.

So Peter climbed out of the boat and tried to copy Jesus. But when the wind began to buffet him this way and that, and the great waves hurled themselves at him, his courage failed and he began to sink. "Lord, save me!" he shouted. And Jesus immediately caught him by the hand, saying, "Peter, how little your faith is. Why did you have any doubts?"

Together they got back into the boat, and the great storm died away completely. The disciples knelt down and worshipped Jesus. "You really are the Son of God," they said.

Later that day they landed at a place called Gennesaret. As soon as people knew who had arrived, they came flocking to him, bringing all their sick friends and relations. They believed they only needed to touch the hem of Jesus' robe to be made well again. And that is exactly what happened.

Matthew 14; Mark 6; John 6.

DEAR GOD, be good to me.
The sea is so wide,
and my boat is so small.

The Breton Fisherman's Prayer

Others there are who go to sea in ships
    and make their living on the wide waters.
These men have seen the acts of the Lord
    and his marvellous doings in the deep.
At his command the storm wind rose
    and lifted the waves high.
So they cried to the Lord in their trouble,
    and he brought them out of their distress.
The storm sank to a murmur
    and the waves of the sea were stilled.
Let them thank the Lord for his enduring love
    and for the marvellous things he has done for men.

from Psalm 107

THEY WANTED TO SEE JESUS

Once, when Jesus was on his way to Jerusalem, he heard a loud voice crying his name. It was a blind beggar called Bartimaeus who'd asked people in the crowd what all the fuss was about. "Why, Jesus of Nazareth is passing by," they had told him, and the minute he heard that he yelled at the top of his voice, "Jesus, Son of David, have mercy on me!"

Those at the front of the crowd ordered him to be quiet but he only shouted more loudly, "Son of David, have mercy on me!"

Jesus stopped and commanded those nearby to bring Bartimaeus to him. "What do you want me to do for you?" he asked.

"Lord, let me see," the poor man pleaded.

"Receive your sight," Jesus told him. "Your faith has healed you." At once the man could see and he followed the Master, glorifying God for the great miracle.

Soon afterwards Jesus was passing through Jericho. There was a very rich man in that city called Zacchaeus, a tax collector. He wanted to see Jesus too, but he was very short

and the heads of the crowd were in the way. Nobody let him through; they didn't like tax collectors very much.

So he ran on ahead and climbed up into a sycamore tree, knowing that Jesus would pass right underneath. When Jesus reached the tree he looked up into the branches and saw the little man hanging there, looking eagerly down.

"Hurry up and climb out of there, Zacchaeus," he said. "I'm coming to stay at your house today."

Zacchaeus scrambled down, overjoyed, but the crowd muttered, "Huh, Jesus has gone to stay at the house of a wicked greedy man."

But the tax collector knew he had done bad things. "Lord," he told Jesus, "I'm going to give half my goods to the poor, and if I've cheated anyone, I'll give them four times what I owe."

Jesus said, "Today salvation has come to this house. I, the Son of man, have come to find what is lost, and to save it." That day, Zacchaeus was truly saved.

Mark 10; Luke 18, 19.

I never saw the moor,
I never saw the sea;
Yet know I how the heather looks,
And what a wave must be.

I never spoke with God,
Nor visited in heaven;
Yet certain am I of the spot
As if a chart were given.

Emily Dickinson

Zacchaeus was a very little man,
And a very little man was he.
He climbed up into a sycamore tree
For the Saviour he wanted to see.
And when the Saviour passed that way,
He looked into the tree and said:
"Now, Zacchaeus, you come down,
For I'm coming to your house for tea."

from Junior Praise

22

LOST AND FOUND

The ordinary folk loved Jesus dearly but the rich and powerful ones were jealous. "He spends too much time with bad people," they muttered. "He sits and eats with liars and cheats. We don't understand it at all."

"Let me explain," Jesus said. "If you had a hundred sheep and one of them wandered away, wouldn't you leave the ninety-nine safe in their pasture and go hunting for the lost one until you found it? When you had, you would lift it up on to your shoulders and carry it home in triumph; then you would call all your friends and neighbours together and say, 'Look at this, I've found my lost sheep. Let's have a party.' What I'm saying is that there will be more joy in heaven over a sinner who says he's sorry than over the good people who don't need to." And to show them exactly what he meant he told them a story about a man and his two sons.

The younger son liked having a good time, and one day he said to his father, "I want my share of your property *now*." The father agreed and divided what he had between his two sons. A few days later the younger son left home and settled in a land far away, where he spent the money on drinking and gambling. In no time at all he had used up every penny.

When his pockets were empty a dreadful famine spread over the countryside and very soon he began to need food. So he went to work for one of the local landowners who packed him off into one of his fields, to feed the pigs. He was now so hungry that he would have been quite glad to eat some of the pig swill. But nobody gave him a thing.

In the end he came to his senses. "My father's servants back home have more food than they can eat," he told himself, "and here I sit, about to collapse with hunger. I will get up this minute and go to my father and I'll say to him, 'Father, I've sinned against God and against you too. I'm not fit to be called your son any more. Treat me as one of your hired servants'." And he got up and started for home.

But his father saw him while he was still a long way from the house, and his heart went out to him. He ran towards him with arms outstretched, flung them round the boy's neck and kissed him. "Father," the son said, thoroughly bewildered, "I've sinned against God and I've sinned against you as well. I'm not fit to be called 'son' any more. Treat me as one of your hired servants."

But his father seemed not to be listening; he was too busy giving orders. "Bring the best robe," he commanded, "and put it on my son. Put a ring on his finger and shoes on his feet, then go and kill my prize calf. We're going to have a feast. My 'dead' son is alive again, my 'lost' son has been found." And everyone began to celebrate.

Now the older one had been out working in the fields and as he walked back he heard music and dancing. When the servants explained what was going on, he was so angry he refused to go in.

Out came the father and begged his son to join them, but he was still in a rage. "Look," he pointed out, "I've slaved for you all these years and I've never once disobeyed you. But you never killed a prize beast for me, no, not so much as a goat kid, so I could feast with my friends. But the minute *he* turns up, having squandered all the money you gave him, you go and kill the prize calf. It's not fair."

"My son," said his father, "you are always with me, and whatever I have is yours. But how could we not rejoice on such a happy day? Your brother, whom I'd given up for dead, is alive and well. I thought he was lost, but he's been found."

And in the same way, Jesus told the people round him, the angels of God sing aloud for joy when one sinner comes home, saying he is sorry.

Luke 15.

THE MAN ON A DONKEY

Once, a clever lawyer who had been listening to Jesus' stories decided to try and trick him. "Teacher," he asked, "what must I do if I want to live for ever in God's Kingdom?"

"What does it say in the Scriptures?" Jesus answered.

"It says that you must love God with all your heart, with all your soul, with all your mind and with all your strength. After that you must love your neighbour as much as you love yourself."

"You're right," Jesus told him. "Do this and you will have everlasting life."

But the lawyer wasn't satisfied. "Who *is* my neighbour?" was his next question.

"There was once a man travelling from Jerusalem to Jericho," Jesus said, "and on a lonely stretch of road some robbers attacked him. They stripped him, beat him up and went off leaving him half dead.

"Now as it happened a priest soon came along the same bit of road. But when he saw the poor man lying there, he simply crossed over to the other side. Some time later another priest, a Levite this time, also came walking along. He did exactly the same thing, just crossed the road and hurried on his way.

"Eventually a Samaritan rode up, someone you wouldn't expect to be any help at all. But when he saw the man, pity filled his heart. He went straight over to him, poured oil and wine on to his wounds and bandaged them up; then he lifted the poor man on to his own donkey and took him to the nearest inn where he looked after him all night.

"In the morning the Samaritan took out his purse and gave the innkeeper some money. 'Take care of him,' he said, 'and if you spend any more than this, I'll pay you when I come back.'

"Now which of these three people was 'neighbour' to the man who had been attacked by robbers?" Jesus asked.

"The one who was kind to him," the clever lawyer replied.

"Go and do as he did, then," said Jesus.

Luke 10.

LORD of the loving heart,
May mine be loving too.
Lord of the gentle hands,
May mine be gentle too.
Lord of the willing feet,
May mine be willing too.
So may I grow more like thee
In all I say and do.

Unknown

THEY ALL RAN AWAY

When Jesus rode into Jerusalem, on a little donkey, crowds lined the streets, with everybody cheering and waving palm branches. But this made the important men of the city, the chief priests and the scribes and the rulers of the Temple, very frightened. The people were flocking to Jesus in such large numbers that they feared he would become the ruler instead of them, perhaps even a king. These jealous men did not understand that when Jesus spoke of his 'kingdom', he meant the Kingdom of God. They decided that they must get rid of him, once and for all.

Jesus already knew that they were planning to put him to death. It said so in the ancient Scriptures which he had read and studied since he was a child.

On the night before the chief priests came to arrest him, he went with his disciples to the Mount of Olives. "Before very long, Peter," he said to his oldest friend, "you will deny that you ever knew me."

"Never!" Peter reassured him, and so did all the others.

"Yes," Jesus repeated, "before the cock crows you will

deny me three times." He knew that they would all be very frightened when the men came to take him away.

Then he told his friends to keep watch, while he went away by himself, to pray. But it was very late and, one by one, they all fell asleep. "Couldn't you stay awake for a single hour?" he said to them, when he found them all lying on the ground; then he returned to his prayers. But the second time he came back, and the third, he found them fast asleep again. "Still sleeping?" he said to them as they all got up, heavy-eyed, not knowing what to say. "Come, make yourselves ready. The traitor is here." People were making their way through the darkness with lanterns, looking for him.

It was Judas, one of his own disciples, who had brought these people to Jesus, and they had paid him thirty pieces of silver for doing so. Up they came, armed with swords and clubs, as if Jesus were some kind of robber. Judas had arranged a secret sign, to show them whom to arrest. "I will kiss him," he had told them.

"Hail, Master," he said, putting his arms round Jesus, and they immediately closed in and grabbed him.

"Do you betray the Son of man with a kiss?" Jesus asked his disciple. Then the rest of his disciples ran off in terror, and Jesus was taken away to Caiaphas, the High Priest. But Peter stayed, following at a distance, to see what was going to happen.

He sat in the courtyard, warming himself by the fire there, while they asked Jesus all kinds of questions, in an attempt to trick him, but Peter noticed that his Master hardly answered a word. While they were questioning him they spat at him, and struck him across the face.

A maid came up to Peter and said, "You were one of Jesus' friends, weren't you?" But Peter shook his head. "I'm sure this man was with Jesus of Nazareth," she told the people standing by. But Peter swore that he was not. "But you were," they all said, "we can tell from the way you speak."

"I do not know the man," Peter said savagely. And immediately the cock crowed.

Then the Lord turned round, and looked at Peter, and he remembered what had been said on the Mount of Olives, that before the cock crowed he would deny Jesus three times. And he went out, and wept bitterly.

Mathew 21, 26; Mark 11, 14; Luke 19, 22; John 12, 18.

A Prayer from Prison

Lord Jesus Christ
You were poor and in distress,
a captive and forsaken as I am.
You know all man's troubles;
You abide with me
when all men fail me;
You remember and seek me;
It is your will that I should know you
and turn to you.
Lord, I hear your call and follow;
Help me. AMEN

Dietrich Bonhoeffer

THE GREAT DARKNESS

In the morning the rulers of the Temple decided that Jesus must die. So they dragged him in front of Pontius Pilate, a Roman governor who was in charge of Jerusalem and of the lands round about. "Are you the King of the Jews?" he said.

"You say I am," Jesus replied. But apart from that he said nothing at all.

Now at that time it was the great feast of the Passover, when it was the custom for the governor to set a prisoner free. The people were allowed to choose who it should be. In the jail there was a wicked man called Barabbas. Pilate asked them if they wanted him to go free. Or would they prefer Jesus?

While he was discussing it with them, his wife sent him a message. "Have nothing to do with that innocent man Jesus," it said. "In my dreams last night I was deeply troubled because of him." But the people who had brought Jesus to the governor were quite determined to have him killed. "Let him be crucified!" they all shouted.

"Why? What has he done wrong?" Pontius Pilate asked them. But they just shouted, "Crucify him!" louder and louder. In the end he had to let Barabbas go free, and Jesus was taken away.

Then it was the turn of the Roman soldiers. They made him wear a kingly robe, to mock him, and they pushed a crown of thorns down on to his head. They put a cane in his hand, pretending it was a royal sceptre, then they hit him and jeered at him, until the time had come for him to be taken out to be crucified.

The custom was that each man carried his own cross up to the hill of Golgotha (which means 'place of a skull'). But

Jesus stumbled and fell, so they got a man called Simon of Cyrene to carry it for him. When they had nailed Jesus to his cross they sat round arguing about who should get his clothes. They couldn't agree, so in the end they threw dice, to decide.

Two robbers were crucified with Jesus, one on each side of him. One hurled insults at him. "If you really are the Christ," he said, "then save yourself, and save us too." But the other rebuked him. "Don't you fear God?" he said. "You got the same sentence as he did. So did I, and we both deserved it. But this man has done nothing wrong at all." Then he said, "Lord Jesus, remember me when you come into your Kingdom."

"Today, you will be with me in paradise," said the Lord.

At about twelve o'clock, as the three of them hung dying, there was a sudden darkness over the whole earth. It lasted for three long hours, and in the Temple the holy curtain was split in two, from the top to the bottom. Then Jesus cried out, "Father, into your hands I give my spirit." And he died.

When the Roman officer who was on watch saw what had happened, he was filled with wonder. "Truly," he said to himself, "this man was the Son of God."

Matthew 27; Mark 15; Luke 23; John 18–19.

Were you there when they crucified my Lord?
Were you there when they crucified my Lord?
Oh, sometimes it causes me to tremble, tremble, tremble;
Were you there when they crucified my Lord?

Were you there when they nailed him to the tree?
Were you there when they nailed him to the tree?
Oh, sometimes it causes me to tremble, tremble, tremble;
Were you there when they nailed him to the tree?

Were you there when they laid him in the tomb?
Were you there when they laid him in the tomb?
Oh, sometimes it causes me to tremble, tremble, tremble;
Were you there when they laid him in the tomb?

Traditional

When I survey the wondrous Cross
On which the Prince of Glory died,
My richest gain I count but loss,
And pour contempt on all my pride.

Isaac Watts

35

THE GREAT SUN

When evening came a rich man called Joseph, from Arimathaea, who had also been a follower of Jesus, went to Pontius Pilate and asked if he could have the Lord's body. It was given to him and he took it away, wrapped it in clean fresh linen then laid it in a tomb cut out of the rock. Then he rolled a huge stone across the entrance, and went away. Mary Magdalene, who had once anointed Jesus with oil, and Mary, the sister of his friend Lazarus, sat watching.

Meanwhile, the men who had him put to death went to Pontius Pilate themselves. "Sir," they said, "when he was alive that liar Jesus of Nazareth claimed that three days after his execution he would rise from the dead. You ought to make sure the tomb is properly guarded, just in case his disciples steal the body, then tell the people he has risen."

"You may have some soldiers," Pontius Pilate told them. "Go and make it as secure as you can." So they went off to the tomb, sealed the stone all round and set a guard to keep watch.

Early in the morning of the third day the two Marys went back to see Jesus' grave. Suddenly there was a tremendous earthquake and an angel came down from heaven. He rolled back the enormous stone and sat on it. His face was like lightning and his robes were as white as snow. When they saw him, the guards shook in terror and fell down, fainting.

Then the angel said to the two women, "Do not be afraid. I know you are looking for Jesus, who was crucified. He is not here, he has risen, just as he promised. Look, this is where his body lay.

"Now go quickly and tell his disciples that he has indeed

risen from the dead and gone on ahead into Galilee. You will see him there. This is the message I was sent to give you."

Still nervous, but with great joy in their hearts, the women hurried away from the tomb and ran to find the disciples. Suddenly Jesus met them on the path. He greeted them and they fell down on their faces before him, and clasped his feet.

"Do not be afraid," he said, "but tell my friends that they must go to Galilee. They will see me there, up on the mountainside."

So the disciples made their way to Galilee, to the place where Jesus had said he would meet them. There he was, just as he had promised, and when they were all gathered together he gave them a special command.

"God my Father has given me full power," he told them, "in heaven and on earth. Your task is to go out and find disciples among every nation, baptizing them in the name of the Father and the Son and the Holy Spirit, teaching them to obey all the things I have commanded you.

"And remember, I am with you always, even unto the end of the world."

Matthew 27–28.

There are also many other things which Jesus did. If they were all to be put down, I suppose the earth itself could not contain all the books that would be written.

John 21.

Once Upon A Time

Once upon a time there lived a man who was a miracle,
Once upon a time there grew a man like God;
All the people came to him to listen to his teaching,
Children gladdened at his touch, and men grew good.

Blind girls blinked their eyes awake and saw the world all coloured;
Crooked men stood straight as trees, alive and strong;
Lonely people lifted up their hearts like flowers to sunshine,
Crippled children danced for joy, and dumb boys sang.

Always I am with you, said this man who was a miracle,
I will never leave you till the seas run dry;
Listen for me, look for me, and you will surely find me;
And the wonder of my touch will bring you joy.

M. E. Rose

*That in his light
we may see light.*